A Teacher's Gift

*Ten Timeless Stories That Caused
Extraordinary Impact*

David L. Thomas

A Teacher's Gift
Ten Timeless Stories
That Caused Extraordinary Impact

© 2009 by David L. Thomas

❧ *www.aTeachersGift.com*

Book cover and layout designed by
Creative Stream Marketing
www.CreativeStreamMarketing.com

ISBN: 978-1-61584-111-0

Printed in China

Dedication

I dedicate this book to the wonderful and amazing people who have devoted their lives to the noble profession of teaching.

You may never know this side of heaven the number of lives you have inspired by your example and through your encouragement.

Acknowledgements

My desire and dream to write a book honoring teachers who have blessed my life would never have become a reality without the dedication of an amazing team of people.

To my beautiful wife Kathie, you caught my attention in junior high by throwing a paper wad at me and have kept my attention ever since. I love you now more than ever!

Our personal assistant, Emma Byler, who fills the many gaps in our lives with her giftedness and heart to serve.

Michelle DeFabio, a highly-respected teacher, friend, and gifted writer. She took my fragmented memories of teachers who influenced and inspired me and labored to the point that a book was birthed.

Mike and Michele Bower and Wade Stankich of MCW Inc. who brought such creativity and giftedness to the table from so many angles.

❧ *www.mcw-inc.com*

John Centofanti of Creative Stream Marketing whose skills, experience, and expertise helped bring this project to its conclusion.

❧ *www.CreativeStreamMarketing.com*

I so appreciate my team who is dedicated to the vision of honoring teachers and recognizing the impact they have made in the lives of many.

Contents

Foreword

I can vividly recall walking in the parking lot wearing a black suit and twirling my keys with my finger. It was a beautiful day in Northeastern Ohio. The kind where the sun shines so brightly that one's view is obstructed. I entered the door and shook the hand of a friendly greeter who escorted me into the auditorium. I quickly found a seat in the back row... a perfect spot for my first visit.

Within moments, the strum of the guitar played and hundreds of people stood to their feet to sing along to the words displayed on the screen. Being a first-time visitor, I'm sure you can imagine the half-hearted singing I was doing while trying to scope out this new place.

At every turn, people were smiling with voices shouting out. However, one voice stood out among the rest...

"Good morning, Victory Christian Center! How is everybody doing?"

"Good morning, Pastor," shouted the congregation.

"Why don't you turn around and hug on someone before we get started."

Before I knew it, I was getting hugs and handshakes from all around me. After a few moments, people took their places and Pastor Thomas began his message. I don't recall all of the points of his teaching, but I do remember the bottom line: *We have power; we can change people through our acts and words; we can change ourselves.*

I pulled out of the parking lot that day and knew there was no need for a second interview. Victory Christian Center became my home church for the next four years and Pastors David and Kathie Thomas became my friends. I honestly can not recall a time being in the presence of Pastor Thomas without walking away a better person.

It isn't because he delivers a teaching each time we shake hands. It's because he chooses to use the power he has, the power we all have, to speak life, to encourage, to make a difference within the shortest of exchanges. No. He doesn't give a sermon every time I see him, he doesn't have to... his message is delivered in the way he lives.

I've had the privilege of working with Pastor Thomas as his dream for this book unfolded into what you are holding in your hand. From the first word scribed to the final edit, the vision and purpose of this book has been to honor teachers and to encourage all of us to activate the power within us to make a change. To change the life of a person, a community, a generation.

Pastor Thomas had teachers who recognized that power and demonstrated it to a young man who has never forgotten the gift that was given to him. Being a teacher, I am inspired to do the same for my students. As you journey through the memories captured in these stories, you will be moved by the simplicity of the message: One gesture, one word, one person. Each can make a difference that lasts a lifetime. Enjoy!

Michelle DeFabio

1
Good, Better, Best

Mrs. Kimble was among one of my very favorite teachers. I hope we all have that small handful of teachers that we remember and perhaps even get choked up about when we think of the impact he or she has made in our lives. As I write this, I can actually recapture some of the moments that Mrs. Kimble made me laugh, smile, and even question.

However, what I really remember are the core values she taught me at such a young age. I know what you may be thinking, David Thomas didn't have parents that could teach him what was important and so he *needed* a Mrs. Kimble. That couldn't be further from the truth.

I was blessed with wonderful, loving parents. To be honest, my parents taught me many of the same core values that I learned from my teachers, but like you, I can't explain the phenomenon that happens when a child seamlessly understands from a stranger what their parents have been telling them for years. This phenomenon has made me realize how significant my teachers were in my life, especially Mrs. Kimble.

I have been a pastor for over 30 years. Every day I interact with people. I encourage them to love God completely, love people unconditionally and love life enthusiastically. I have realized throughout my ministry that some of these core values that I hold dear to my heart were modeled for me by people who were positioned in my life to influence me, my teachers. If you are reading this book and you are a teacher, I would like to share my heart with you for a moment.

My heart has been imprinted upon by my teachers from first grade through high school.

Teachers have been such a gift in my life. My heart has been imprinted upon by my teachers from first grade through high school. I am so amazed by the calling on your life to be a teacher. The vision for this book has been to show appreciation for the life of service you have given to your students and their families.

Dream big for your students when they have lost their own dream.

Through you, your students' lives are being changed every day. You responded to a call to be a teacher and this book is a gift to thank you for saying yes. With the stories that you read it is my hope and prayer that you feel encouraged to dream big for your students when they have lost their own dream, that you continue to encourage and speak life into them when they feel discouraged and helpless and most of all, when you feel discouraged, that you persevere. No matter what you may see or hear, you are making a difference in the lives of your students.

You are impacting their lives. You are impacting the world. Like Mrs. Kimble taught me in second grade, "Good, better, best... never let it rest until the good is better and the better is best." Much of what others admire about me I learned from a teacher who pulled out the best in me.

I am forever grateful that they never rested with my good or better until I became my best. This book is a gift to say thank you for not resting. As you read the following stories from my life, I hope you see yourself in my teachers and you see me in your students. I honor you for what you do, and thank you again for saying yes. I will be forever grateful!

2
That's Not the Real Santa!

I can still see Mrs. Miller as she stood in front of our first grade classroom with the man she considered to be Santa Claus. However, she had David Thomas in her class, the Santa Claus expert. After all, I was the veteran first grader!

Being held back, I knew the routine beyond the rookies in the room. I could spot from a mile away that he wasn't the real deal. There was no way she was going to be able to pull the wool over these eyes; in all my expertise I had to let her know. I mean, what was she thinking, with that yellow string hanging down from the side of his face?

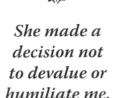

She made a decision not to devalue or humiliate me.

It was my obligation to all Santa Claus believers to call him out, so I did. My hand shot up, "Mrs. Miller, this isn't the real Santa! He has a gold string holding up his beard!"

I'm sure the entire class gasped as did the jolly red-suited man. I can still see the big frown on Mary, my fellow classmate's face. Her generally smiling countenance was now screaming, "How in the world could you have done that?"

However, Mrs. Miller did something absolutely brilliant. She graciously smiled at me and grabbed a pair of scissors from her desk. She walked over to the gentleman, masterfully cut the gold string to avoid letting the cat out of the bag, and attempted to demonstrate to the rookies that his beard was real and this was in fact the real Santa.

I didn't buy it, but you could imagine what I was anticipating. I mean, what child would get away with doing what I did? However, Mrs. Miller was amazing. She didn't embarrass me or scold me. She knew my heart. I was a child doing a childish act, not a rebellious one.

Mrs. Miller taught me about grace that day. She didn't give me what I might have deserved. To put it bluntly, Mrs. Miller allowed me to save face in front of my classmates and more importantly, Santa Claus. She made a decision not to devalue or humiliate me. She protected me from being the one responsible for telling twenty-five kids that Santa wasn't real, but most of all she preserved my childlike innocence. Mrs. Miller saw beyond the opportunity to scold me; she saw the bigger picture.

I hope each of us can model what my first grade teacher did for me, seeing the bigger picture and choosing to respond to others with something that is eternal. I will always be grateful for that day. It's amazing to me that out of all the time I spent with Mrs. Miller, that is my most vivid memory. It wasn't a spectacular lesson, an outstanding report card, or a Valentine's Day party.

No, the most memorable thing from that year happened in one instant. I encourage you to take advantage of those moments in your classroom when you have the opportunity to see beyond the lesson and impart something into your students. After all, grace is eternal and as with me, those lessons happen in a moment but last a lifetime.

3
The Gift of a Second Chance

What does every child care about in first grade? You got it! I had the coolest Davy Crocket lunch box you could imagine! I can tell you all of my favorite things about first grade but two stand out... my lunch box, of course, and the party my taste buds would throw when my mother would surprise me with my favorite snack... Cheetos™!

I think my fingers still bare an orange-colored hue. Believe it or not, these cheese twists almost became the death of me in first grade, so I thought. Mrs. Miller was teaching us how important proper hygiene was for the past month. I'm sure this was no small task to teach a group of six year olds.

However, as always, she managed to get us excited about each new adventure in learning. Being that this was a new endeavor for this veteran first grader, I took this unit very seriously. As you could imagine, I didn't want to devote another year of my life to first grade. For a month, it was part of my nightly routine to check and double-check my fingers as I gazed at them with a small scrub brush in hand trying to get rid of the results of an active boy raised in rural Ohio.

The teacher announced that she was going to inspect our hands the next day to check for clean, trimmed nails and everything else that goes with a hand inspection. Of course, being the compliant child that I was, I was thrilled to pass the inspection in order to acquire my next shiny, red star for the day! I woke up the next morning and remembered what Mrs. Miller had said. I washed my hands perfectly, gave myself my own inspection and envisioned my red star the entire bus ride to school.

I pondered if this one act would seal my fate as the longest running student in first grade.

As we filed into the classroom, we went on with our daily activities and continued our lessons until lunch. When Mrs. Miller dismissed us , I was eager to crack open my lunch box and begin enjoying my snack!

I looked up at my teacher, the judge of all judges, and in one second the atmosphere changed.

As I was gleefully munching on my Cheetos™, a sense of dread came over me as I looked at my stain-colored fingers. I saw myself looking down a double-barreled gun as I pondered if this one act would seal my fate as the longest running student in first grade. Mrs. Miller specifically said she was going to check each student's fingernails one at a time. Upon feeling bewildered, I began to do what any child would do in that situation. I stuck each finger in my mouth and frantically tried to lick off all the cheese. I must admit as I think about that day, they were finger lickin' good!

Lunch time was over and now the moment I was dreading was coming closer. As Mrs. Miller drew nearer, I could feel myself fighting back the tears. Before she could say anything, I cried out, "When I came to school, my hands were clean!"

I looked up at my teacher, the judge of all judges, and in one second the atmosphere changed. The sun came out and the world was OK again when she simply said to me, "David, let's wash your hands."

Wash my hands? That's my sentencing? I get to wash my hands? Amazing. Mrs. Miller wasn't going to scold me or take away all of my stickers because of one inspection gone bad. No, she extended to me something so profound... a second chance.

We all have the opportunity to be on both sides of the fence, in the position of the judge or as the soon-to-be-judged. This incident taught me about "The Golden Rule;" Mrs. Miller taught me about second chances. She didn't have to sit me down and teach it to me, she just extended it to me. Because of her, I've learned to focus on the solution rather than the problem.

This core value has taught me to respond to people and situations rather than react to them. In this case, soap and water became my saving grace. Mrs. Miller looked for the solution. I'm sure we can all recount a moment in time when we desperately hoped and prayed that someone would let a mistake slide and give us a break... our boss, spouse, friend, credit card company... the list is endless.

Mrs. Miller gave me a break with that inspection. She also taught me a great lesson of being a solution-oriented rather than a problem-oriented person.

As teachers, I encourage you to look at the simplicity of a second chance with your students. Who knows, you might need them to extend one to you someday.

4
Sticks and Stones

We can all recite the mantra, "Sticks and stones may break my bones, but words will never hurt me." I'm not sure who coined this phrase, but I have thought many times in my mind that I'd much rather recover from a few bruises than suffer from the sting of one hurtful word.

It would be painful, but each of us could go back to our elementary days and recall a time when a classmate hurt our feelings with their words. It seems as though that's when a part of our innocence is lost. We realize for the first time that people we care about can hurt us. Mrs. Colla, however, knew the power of words and taught this man back in first grade to never allow anyone to steal one of the most important possessions we have, self-love.

Flashcards, practicing penmanship, reciting, "*I* before *e*, except after *c*," it was a typical day at Hartford Elementary School. Mrs. Colla got through her morning lessons and we were headed to the part of the day we looked forward to the most. It's the time when children's hearts are screaming, "Set the captives free!" Recess!

She knew the power of words. She was intent in never having one of us fall victim to them.

Don't we all wish we still had a designated time to just be a kid? Let's face it; recess is where it all happened. The girls went to one side of the playground to play school, which was a mystery to the boys. We finally get a break from school and the girls want to play school. The boys found any object that would bounce and started up a crazy game that never seemed to end. While the sweat was dripping down my brow, I was astonished to hear Mrs. Colla blow the whistle to end recess.

There was no way! No one had won the game! It was too early to go back to science class and learn about evaporation. The only thing that seemed to be evaporating was my fun.

However, Mrs. Colla was not one to listen to moaning and groaning. She blew the whistle and we came running. She lined us up and walked us into the classroom. When we entered, she asked us to sit quietly in our seats. I could tell we were gearing up for something other than a science lesson. Mrs. Colla had brought us in early because she had heard a student call a classmate a name. What name? I'm not sure, but it didn't matter.

To Mrs. Colla, any word that hurt anyone was unacceptable. My palms began to sweat as we all sat in the room and listened to Mrs. Colla talk to us about the situation. I thought to myself, what punishment is she going to give? A phone call home? Oh, boy, I could only imagine what my father would do if I... forget it... I wasn't going to go there. But true to form, Mrs. Colla didn't even raise an eyebrow.

She looked each of us in the eyes and declared with an authority a message I can still remember. Her sermon: never allow the words spoken out of the

The wise man of old stated that death and life are in the power of the tongue.

mouth of another diminish the way you feel about yourself. She knew the power of words. She was intent in never having one of us fall victim to them.

After all, Solomon, the wise man of old, stated that death and life are in the power of the tongue. It was more important to her to take the opportunity to teach us a life-lesson than expose another student's mistake. I still don't know what word was spoken, who said it, or who the victim was. I just remember Mrs. Colla's eyes. She looked at me like I was a prince and taught me that it would be criminal to believe anything else.

I have the power within myself to build someone up or tear them down, we all do. Every day I am given opportunities to exercise this power. What I say is going to make an impact in another's life. I determine if it's going to bring life or not. My elementary teacher blew that whistle and dragged a group of twenty-five school kids off the playground. Not because she had to simply teach us a lesson. No, she had to teach us a lesson about who we are, what we have, and what we're worth. I can't think of a better lesson she taught. I can't think of a better gift I've received.

Teachers have these awesome opportunities everyday. Seeing beyond the lesson to teach a lesson is a gift and Mrs. Colla had it. She encouraged each of us to be mindful of the words we spoke because they had power. She also expected us to not believe words that said we were less than who we believed to be, who she believed us to be.

My life was transformed by the words that were spoken to me as a child.

If you are reading this book and can envision your students, imagine for a moment what the world would be like if classrooms were filled with a standard that preserved the healthy self-love Mrs. Colla encouraged. Imagine yourself speaking to your students and encouraging them to see themselves as princes and princesses. If you can imagine it, you can do it. My first grade teacher had this gift, but you do too. You have the power to create a generation that thinks of themselves as royalty.

My life was transformed by the words that were spoken to me as a child sitting in a Hartford Elementary classroom. Mrs. Colla looked at me like I was a prince and some odd years later, I'm sticking to it. Sticks and stones may break my bones, but fewer words are going to hurt me, thanks to Mrs. Colla.

5
She Made Me Feel Like Michelangelo

It's impossible to create this gift for teachers without thinking of Mrs. Santelli. My heart swells while remembering how she made me feel while sitting in her classroom. I'm sure everyone has a favorite teacher, but Mrs. Santelli, my third grade teacher, well; I'll let you read for yourself.

There I sat at my desk while Mrs. Santelli described the art project that the class would be working on to capture the holiday season, a winter mural to be displayed in the hallway for the entire school to see.

As always, she had us jumping out of our seats with excitement as she described each detail of the project.

All we needed was the nod of our teacher's head, and we were off. My friend Mike and I sat on the floor with every colored crayon a nine year old could imagine. I can still smell the crayons from the big 64-count box I had with, may I add, its own sharpener built in! While Mike worked his magic on one end, I was on the other. I remember drawing a bright, yellow sun and mountains along the top of the ten-foot butcher paper. While biting my tongue as I made sure to stay within the lines I had drawn, Mrs. Santelli observed my efforts.

Looking back, I'm sure my artistic ability was a step past stick figures, but Mrs. Santelli didn't see that at all. She bent down next to me; looked at my art work, and then asked me to do something I have never forgotten. She asked me to sign my name. I couldn't believe she wanted me to autograph my work. At that moment she made me feel like Michelangelo. I'm sure I wasn't as good as she led on, but she saw a gift in me and that has made a major difference in my

She was granting me the gift we each need; the gift of encouragement.

life. What I have learned since that day is that she was granting me the gift we each need; the gift of encouragement.

A teacher believing in me was the greatest gift I ever received at such a young, impressionable age. Every one of us needs to have someone to believe in us, to encourage us, to cheer us on! Teachers do this every day in the most subtle ways. In reality, my art work wasn't important to Mrs. Santelli, I was.

Throughout the year, Mrs. Santelli made an effort to pull out the gifts in me and have me realize them for myself. I believed I was an artist and even sent in a picture of a turtle that I drew into an art contest. I didn't win, but I didn't care. The important thing is that I believed I could. I encourage any educator that is reading this story to see the gold in your students. It's difficult at times, I'm sure. Realizing the awesome opportunity you have been given to speak into a child's life is amazing. Each of you is a treasure and I encourage you to find the gifts that are stored in your students and then offer them the gift we all need, encouragement.

Gold was discovered in me that day, and I couldn't be the person I am today if I wasn't simply asked many years ago to sign my name to my yellow sun.

6
Orange Pop

The stories that cover the pages of this book have illustrated defining moments in my life created by teachers; however, it would be impossible to write this tribute without honoring two of the best teachers I have ever had, my parents.

Lester Thomas, a World War II vet wounded in Okinawa; a welder by trade, a hard-working family man. Like the many teachers I have written about, my father changed my life in one moment. My father grew up in a coal mining town in Pennsylvania. His dad had suffered a head injury during a coal mining accident. As a result of his injury, my dad wasn't able to have the kind of relationship with his father that young boy's desire. Needless to say, communication for my dad was a bit of a struggle. Amazingly enough, I always knew how my father felt about me. He showed me through many means how much he loved me.

It was very typical for my Dad to play catch or even a game of baseball with my friends and me in the backyard after a long day of work. That meant the world to me. As a youngster who loved baseball more than life, I grew up thinking, as many of my friends did, that I was going to be the next Mickey Mantle. I know most young boys grow up thinking they are going to be the next Mickey Mantle, but I really was! I would have played ball in the middle of a tornado. Dad knew my passion for the game and for that reason it was his passion too. He never missed a Little League game.

I was ten years old playing for the Hartford Optimist Little League team. We were playing a tense game against a team from Fowler, OH. I am still convinced the pitcher was an eighteen year old all-star camouflaged in a Little League jersey. He had a fast-pitch that could peel the paint off a fence. This kid threw one pitch and drilled me so badly that I was awarded first base.

By the time I was up at bat again, my palms were sweating buckets. The not-so-distant memory of the first pitch was still embedded mentally and physically. Let's just say I was certainly speaking in a higher voice pitch by the time I came up for round two. With great fear trembling through my arms, sweat dripping off my brow, I gripped the bat and shut my eyes.

With a prayer rolling off my lips, I gave the best swing I could. A holy hush hovered over the crowd as everyone gazed at the ball hurling through the air. My legs moved faster than the rest of my body could as I saw that ball of leather sail across the home run fence. I can still hear the tens of thousands of fans screaming in the crowd. It didn't matter that they weren't really there. A kid can dream. As I was carried off the field in a haze of glory–*I might still be dreaming*–I received many accolades from my team and coach but the best was yet to come.

By many people's standards my family was poor, but we never saw ourselves that way. Even though there were six kids

This pint-size ten year old looked up at his father at that moment and knew for the very first time how much he was loved.

in my family, we never went without. We were well-fed and had good enough clothes for school and play. Therefore, the moment I am about to describe was even more special because of the sacrifice it took.

After the game, I climbed into my father's black Renault, a stick-shift that took a beating when I turned sixteen. Dad kicked on the ignition to get us home. However, on the way to our house, my father made an unexpected stop. With the flip of his blinker we pulled into Miller's Sohio gas station. As Dad and I walked through the front door of the gas station, there Mr. Miller sat behind the counter in his car-mechanic attire. We were greeted with a smile as we walked in. My father asked what I wanted, and with an astonished look, I asked Mr. Miller for an orange pop.

Like I said, we weren't poor, but we didn't fancy ourselves with soda too often. As Mr. Miller handed me the bottle of soda, my father placed his hand on my white, wool jersey and said with all the pride in the world, "My son just hit his first home run." This pint-size ten year old looked up at his father at that moment and knew for the very first time how much he was loved. I felt how proud he was of me.

That day Lester Thomas grew ten feet tall in my eyes. And as for me, well in my mind, I grew ten feet tall as well. My dad did more than buy me an orange pop; he purchased something bigger for me, *confidence*. I was worth the sacrifice of an orange pop. It was one thing to get a pat on the back from my coach and teammates,

He slid a few coins across the counter and defined who I am forever.

but my dad did something monumental. He put me on display for anyone to see; He publicly announced my victory. His son hit a home run.

I was worth making a detour to Miller's gas station. That day I learned the power of words and encouragement. My dad infused me with confidence. It would have taken a strong character to convince me that I couldn't make Mickey Mantle eat my dust after I guzzled down that soda.

Over the years I have shared this story to over 100,000 people and every time I tell it, I still get a lump in my throat. I don't know how significant that moment was for my father, but it was a defining moment in my life. Orange pop has never tasted the same since that day. I've never purchased another without being reminded how weighty our words and gestures can be.

What may be inconsequential to one may be life-changing for another. For my father, Miller's Sohio gas station was his classroom for a moment. He slid a few coins across the counter and defined who I am forever.

I now live my life to help others feel ten feet tall. I hope to give others many orange pop moments. Like my father, I don't teach in the classroom and contrary to popular opinion, teachers don't live in their classrooms. Every day and in every way we all can be a conduit for encouragement and confidence.

Whether you see your students in the mall or at the movies, or if your son or daughter scores the winning point, or perhaps they don't, more importantly, splurge on the orange pop, it's more than just a soda.

7
Discovering Gold

I would imagine if we all think hard and long enough we can remember those particular car rides in which our mom gave us that look through the rearview mirror. It's like a scene from a movie; the half-faced reflection that only allows for the view of the infamous one eyebrow raise. This look got my full attention in one moment, but the lesson she taught has stayed with me for a lifetime.

Although I do not remember tons of these car lessons from mom, the lessons that did come really seemed to stick. In fact, in my great admiration of educators, I have found parents to be the first line of defense in raising healthy kids in what can be an unhealthy world. My parents were not perfect, but they gave their all to provide for me and my five siblings a safe and happy home. I will be eternally grateful to them and have become more amazed at their unconditional love as Kathie and I raised our two children Heather and Dave.

When I do speak about others, if I am not willing to write it and sign it, I'm not willing to say it.

Well, back to the story.

I was a seventh grade boy. Need I say more? In my school this was the first year of Jr. High, the year I began to change classes, the year I played basketball for the Hartford Bobcats, and most importantly, this is the year I met a cute little cheerleader named Kathie Gordon who would one day become my beautiful wife!

This was also the first year of wood shop. The time in which we made the infamous table lamp that was shaped like a wishing well. You know, the kind only a mother could love. This particular fall evening, mom was driving us home from my school's open house. The official meet and greet where parents had opportunity to give the okay to the teacher to do whatever was necessary to keep their sons and daughters in line.

After my mom visited my teachers and saw my classroom, we began to head home. Little did I know that our green Ford Galaxy 500 would be the home of a very special mom moment. I don't remember why I was in such a yackety mood. My mouth was obviously going much faster than my brain's ability to keep up!

I was telling mom about a young girl in our school who was a couple of years younger than me. This girl was a bit larger in size and had the biggest brown eyes I had ever seen with eyelashes that seemed to touch her forehead. They were beautiful, but unusually long. One day I glanced at her and a random image came to my mind. She looked like a cow. Imagine my reaction when it came to me in the middle of the hallway. Worse yet, imagine my mom's reaction when it came out of my mouth. As I was explaining all this with some inappropriate laughter thrown in, I was quickly interrupted with the sound of my full name in a tone that only a mom can give. The next few miles were unforgettable. It was probably good for me that we were only a few miles from home.

In an extremely clear way she let me know that I should never make fun of how another person looks or acts. She was so clear that I find myself squirming in my seat even as I write about these memories! Her reason, you never want to be responsible for bringing pain to another person. I must admit that this young girl's feelings were the furthest thing from my thoughts. I was a seventh grade boy saying whatever came to mind. As I was receiving the mom lesson and a much deserved scolding, I felt like a knucklehead. I was wrong and mom was right.

First of all, I had absolutely no consideration for the other person's feelings. Secondly, why was I telling this to my mom as she had some weight issues of her own? She always jokingly blamed me for ruining her girlish figure. I guess it's hard to recover from having a nine-plus pound baby boy! Looking back, this was one of the first times I realized how much trouble one could get into by choosing the wrong words at the wrong time. At that age I had not yet learned Mark Twain's wit, "The difference between the right word and the almost right word is like the difference between lightning and the lightning bug."

Mom knew she needed to nip this one fast. There was no back-peddling out of this one. I left myself wide open. Mom brought the proper correction, but thankfully she never devalued me.

She taught me that although we are all made in different forms and fashions, it is never proper to say anything to anyone that could bring offense. I learned on that day to be more sensitive to others. When I do speak about others, if I am not willing to write it and sign it, I'm not willing to say it.

I encourage you to follow the path of my mother; never devalue, rather bring out the greatness.

As I spoke at my mom's funeral, these kinds of memories flooded my mind. These are times when only a mom can hold up the mirror in front of us and show us who we really are. Mom taught me that the true skill isn't simply holding up the mirror but showing how to change what is seen. That conversation in the Ford Galaxy transformed my way of thinking.

When others scouted out the weaker kid, more often than not, I rushed to his defense. When picking teams, I overlooked the jock and chose the underdog. Well, at least I thought about it. I do not know if I went from one extreme to the other immediately, but something changed that day. I went from looking at the dirt to looking for the gold.

I give a lot of credit to my mom. She taught me that there is almost always more dirt than gold. Dirt is on the surface, apparent to anyone's eyes, and gold is generally hidden. Only eyes of love can discern the fabulous potential hidden within a person.

Little did I know that I would be granted the privilege of being a public speaker, speaking to people around the world. I assumed that I would work in a factory like almost every man in my family. It was honorable work and provided for many families in our community.

Dirt is on the surface, apparent to anyone's eyes, and gold is generally hidden.

I live my life daily to find great value in those around me. My discovery has been that hurt people tend to hurt people. Much of our unkind words come from a wounded heart. My passion is for bruised and wounded people to be transformed into healthy and life-giving individuals.

For the educator who is standing in front of a sea of children, I challenge you to hold the mirror in front of your students. You may need to bring some correction, but I encourage you to follow the path of my mother. Never devalue, rather bring out the greatness. My mom told me who I was to be during that ride home. She held up a mirror of correction and displayed the dirt and challenged me to let my gold shine.

You have treasures in your room. Go on a treasure hunt and help your students discover their gold. You never know, they may become treasure hunters as well.

8
The Ultimate Challenge

Let's make sure we keep this real. Is there anyone who thinks back to seventh grade and doesn't have to fight back a bit of a gag reflex? I mean really, most of us look back at our school picture and can actually see in the eyes of that twelve year old the agony that went along with being in the height of insecurity, confusion and yes, acne. What we all would have done for a little Pro-Activ™ back in the day.

I struggled with my own insecurity but it was time to separate the men from the boys. Basketball tryouts were open to seventh graders. Only three boys from the grade were to be chosen and I wasn't sure of my plan.

I had a very good reason for never playing basketball in school; it went against my moral code. We had to wear shorts and that was simply not going to happen. I have to admit, I had scrawny legs. However, after some serious consideration I decided to go out for the team. I heard the voices of my past teachers ringing in my head and I realized that I couldn't let fear rule me. I had to overcome this insecurity and I did. Although I was intrinsically driven, I had a little motivation from the sidelines. There was a cute little cheerleader that had caught my eye.

I was feeling muscles I never even knew existed during our basketball practices. Coach had us run drills that seemed to prepare us for war not junior high basketball. One day during a grueling practice Mr. Fox, the school principal, came into the gym. After watching from the sidelines he came to speak to the squad. I knew Mr. Fox a bit more than the others because I was an office helper.

As you can imagine, there were some perks in scoring that position. Mr. Fox gazed at the team and pointed his finger directly at me. Here it was, one of the perks! I puffed out my chest to prepare for the litany of compliments that were sure to follow. However, at the end of his finger shot out a missile when he said, "This kid is the worst defensive player on the whole team." Not *exactly* what I was expecting to hear. I know your heart is probably crushed imagining my little chest concaving as my face turned red. Ironically, that wasn't the case. Mr. Fox was right.

I was a bit of a nightmare on the court, especially on defense. However, I knew what he was up to. I had the fortunate experiences of having teachers pull out the best of me. He pulled out the good ole' reverse psychology card. Be honest, we've all used it. "Susie, no one cleans up the kitchen as good as you. Thank you for helping Mommy."

Sounds familiar, huh? It's an oldie but a goodie and Mr. Fox knew it was what I needed. He presented that statement to me not as condemnation but as a challenge. He knew I was playing below my potential. He saw that I was satisfied with mediocrity and that wasn't acceptable to him. I was capable of more and we both knew it. What may have crushed others motivated me. Mr. Fox established relationship with me; one of the perks I mentioned earlier. He got to know my

You have an all-access pass to challenge your students to become better than they can perceive.

character, my dreams, and my potential. Because of what he did out of relationship, I became the best defensive player by the end of the season.

I understand that Mr. Fox's approach might not be acceptable in today's classrooms; however, I applaud his philosophy. He was in a position of leadership. The only way he was going to be able to speak into my life and challenge me was through influence. He could only influence me through establishing a relationship. Amazing how that works.

I'm sure you have students in your classroom that you see running full steam ahead towards a brick wall. How do you help challenge them to live bigger, live better? What college class prepared you with strategies to accomplish such a task? It might be more than what you bargained for at times, but I want to encourage you to go for it. The investment you make will be worth it.

You are reading stories from my life; stories that changed my course; stories that have made me a better man. My life is changed because my teachers were determined to make a difference in the life of this person. That's why you chose your profession; you wanted to make a difference in your students' lives and let me add, you are qualified to do so.

How can you challenge them to meet their potential? We know it's not through fear and condemnation. As with me, it was through relationship. This is the only way Mr. Fox was able to do what he did. He had permission to challenge me because he had established something with me. You have an all-access pass to

You may be the only one who has the clear lens to see their potential.

challenge your students to become better than they can perceive. You may be the only one who has the clear lens to see their potential. I am living proof.

I am convinced because I was challenged to become a better person and a better player, people became attracted to that passion that was within me to not settle for less. Remember that cute little cheerleader? Since that challenge, she's been cheering me on for over thirty years.

Thank you, Mr. Fox. Thank you for seeing my potential. Thank you for not letting me settle for mediocrity. I am definitely better because of your influence, because of your relationship. You made an investment in me and although it's not possible for you to see it, you would be pleased with the return.

9
Keep Your Eye on the Prize

Cross-country was a means to an end for me during my freshman year. After my seventh grade encounter with Mr. Fox during basketball practice I had worked to secure my position on the basketball team. However, one needed to run cross-country in order to play basketball. Lettering in this sport had become a goal for me; however, in order to letter I had to rank in an event.

It was early in the school year and race day had come. Needless to say, endurance running was not a gift of mine so it was a struggle to get through a race. The whistle blew and we were off. I put my blinders on like a champion horse running out of the gate;

however, about three quarters into the race, I quickly lost stamina as my sides began to split. I wanted to letter so badly, but I convinced myself to give up and attempt to rank in another race. Now would be a good time to introduce you to my friend, Matt. Because he was a good friend of mine, he could tell I was losing steam and heart. Matt caught eyes with me from the sidelines and began to yell my name.

"C'mon, Dave. You can do it! Go! Go!" In that moment I became a Carl Lewis running for the gold. I picked up my pace, pulled back my shoulders and kept my eyes focused on the finish line. Matt cheered me on to the end of that race. Thanks to him, I finished strong and got my letter.

We all need someone to remind us who we are when we get a little tired and weak.

I know this book is about teachers and their influence, but I felt this story really illustrated the ripple effect that teachers can create. The student who encouraged me was emulating our coach. Our cross-country coach really pushed us to believe we could achieve what we thought was impossible. Matt reminded me of that during my race.

Isn't it every teacher's dream to teach something to a student and then watch them become the teacher to another? Matt only did what he saw our coach do. He led me to the finish line through his encouragement and coaching. He saw I was about to give up, and he wouldn't let me do it. He knew I was better than that.

We all need someone to remind us who we are when we get a little tired and weak. Matt knew there was a letter to be earned, a finish line to cross. That day I learned to keep my eye on the prize. The encouragement given to me allowed me to finish strong. I learned this from a coach and a classmate.

I desire for every teacher to know the awesome impact they have in the lives of their students. The ripple effect, what an amazing image; one person does something that affects another and in turn it affects another. It's timeless. It's priceless.

As a pastor I have invested my life in encouraging others to finish strong when their legs get weak. I have a coach to thank for that. Because of his core value of never letting me give up, I am able to coach others and say what was said to me many years ago, "C'mon! You can do it! Go! Go!" I model what they had done to me.

Matt may never know how many lives he has indirectly touched by simply coaching me from the sidelines.

I have had the awesome pleasure to watch many weary runners finish their race, get their letter, achieve their goal. It is my hope that in each of them is the passion to pass on that encouragement. My coach gave it to Matt, Matt gave it to me, and I have passed it on to many.

To the teacher who is reading this story...there is a pebble in your hand. Throw it in the water and watch what will happen. What you do in your classroom, with your students, it's timeless. It's priceless.

10
Not the End of the Story

On graduation day, I threw my cap in the air and marched out of the gym with a smile on my face. I had accomplished it. It was official. My obligation to public education had finally been completed. A feeling of utter victory overcame me. I had put in more time than my peers. Remember, I was the first grade veteran. In moments like those, it seems as though memories flash through our mind like a slide show. I could see myself sitting in Mrs. Kimble's class hearing her sweet voice say, "Good, better, best. Never let it rest until the good is better and the better is best."

What a way to end a journey, remembering the proverbial phrase that your second grade teacher had taught you when bruised knees and spelling tests were the main stressors of life. What a tribute to her, to all of my teachers, to remember such things. I bet if any of them were in that crowd during that ceremony, they were beaming with pride seeing their former students get their diploma. Because of them I made it to that celebration. I may have been off to a rocky start, but because of the impact of my teachers, I made it. I'm sure teachers look at their students' accomplishments and partake of the sweet smell of victory as well. After all, it is their efforts that contribute to such achievement.

I often wish I could get in touch with Mr. Mangione, my senior year government teacher, and tell him who I turned out to be. I'm sure he would be happy for me, however, I would probably be able to knock him over with a feather. A bittersweet memory comes to mind when I reflect back on my government class.

My teacher had given us an assignment to give an oral report. Can you feel my anxiety? They say that public speaking ranks right up there with death when listing what people fear the most. Needless to say, I felt like I died a thousand deaths when I was given the assignment to stand in front of my peers and actually speak! Forget it. Nope. Not going to happen. I was determined to avoid this assignment, and I did. It never did happen. Good ole' David Thomas told the teacher that he wasn't going to be getting up in front of anyone! I was successful in getting my way but paid a price. The alternative assignment, receive a failing grade. I received the "F" for

I often think about how my teacher must have felt. I'm sure he thought he failed me.

my grade, but I managed to pass the class. It really didn't affect my overall grade too much, but make no mistake about it–it affected me in many other ways.

I often think about how my teacher must have felt. I'm sure he thought he failed me. Think about it, a teacher comes face-to-face with a student who says he'd much rather fail than do what the teacher believes is important. All the planning and prep work he did for his students, and I said, "No thanks." In his mind, he couldn't reach me or encourage me. He couldn't plant a seed in me, or so he thought.

I recall the stories of my childhood often and have the opportunity to share them with many. The people I share these stories with range in age, color, and creed. I speak to them via CD, DVD, Podcasts, through all the venues of modern day technology. However, I mostly speak to them vis-à-vis, face-to-face–all 2,500 of them; eyes looking straight at me, listening to the words coming from my mouth and my heart.

Being a preacher to a congregation of such a large size was part of my destiny. My government teacher had no idea of the call on my life. I'm sure he just feels like I was another student that didn't get it. I wish I could tell him that I did. Like so many of us, we feel like our efforts are lost when something or someone doesn't end up the way we had hoped.

My government teacher may have felt defeated that day I refused him, but his efforts weren't lost. He planted seed in me, caused me to persevere through my fears. In the nine months that I had him as a teacher, he may not have seen the fruit he was hoping to see, however, some odd years later, I wish I could tell him that his basket is plentiful.

With this last story, I want to say to you that the seed you plant in your students while they are sitting in your class never dies.

The seed you plant in your students while they are sitting in your class never dies.

You may not see the fruit in the time they are with you, but you are planting something in them. It may take time to grow, it will need pruned and watered, but make no mistake about it, when the bell rings, and the year is over it is not the end of the story. Close this book and know that your basket is plentiful.

11
Thank You for the Gift

We all have stories to tell, stories that are packed with inheritance and promise, stories that have transformed minds and have remained timeless. It is my heart's desire to have shared such stories with you. Being a pastor of a church, I have the amazing opportunity to interact with people on many levels. I counsel, teach, lead, and encourage.

One of my favorite among these is that I get to honor others. One of my greatest pleasures in being a pastor occurs every September. I ask all the teachers in the congregation to join us on the platform so the entire church can see them. At that time my wife and I take the opportunity to look into their eyes and thank and honor them for what they do. I'd like to share with you what I say to them and would be honored to speak the same thing to you.

Teaching is more than a profession, a job, or a career. It is a calling, a high calling to make a mark in a person's life, to set the stage for success, to light the path to one's dreams. For all the lives you have touched, I'd like to thank you. For all the bad moments you have made good, I'd like to thank you. For all the gold you've uncovered, thank you. May you be used to encourage your students to live big and dream bigger. Be inspired to go further and fly higher as you embark on a school year that is greater than the last.

I represent one voice of many to say, "Thank you." Thank you for choosing the distinguished career of teaching. Thank you for your dedication and hard work. Thank you for the difference you make on a regular basis. Today and each day may you have an incredible sense of the healthy pride and accomplishments for the decision to impact the lives of others by being a teacher. May you be used to inspire many in ways that no

May you never lose sight of the incredible impact you are making upon your students.

one else could do but you. May you have a sense of destiny about what you do. May you be able to see the big picture beyond the daily grind that life can bring. May you be able to fill a student's life with wonder and possibility through your belief in that student and your ability to inspire them to believe.

And finally, may you be blessed to know that you are a blessing! May you never lose sight of the incredible impact you are making upon your students. I am one of many thankful and appreciative admirers of those who can gladly say, "I am a teacher."

May God bless you continually,

Pastor David L. Thomas

12
A Teacher's Perspective

I remember sitting in a college auditorium twelve years ago being asked by my professor to write an essay on my mission statement for the classroom. Seriously? What college student is thinking of a mission statement; I wasn't. I was too busy praying for the mission, to survive my first teaching job!

Being a fresh graduate with a degree in elementary education was thrilling and nerve-wracking all at the same time. I couldn't wait to put into practice everything I had learned and yet I was praying I would remember everything I had learned. My mind was filled to capacity with strategies, buzz words, and achievement test standards. I couldn't have been happier. I was ready to make a difference. I know, the cliché of all clichés! But I have to share with you, while my friends were popping popcorn and watching 90210, I was watching the Disney Channel with a box of Puffs™ to see who was going to get the Teacher of the Year Award. I know it's a cliché, but I was going to make a difference. My heart was set on it.

When I graduated from college, I warned my friends not to buy me all the teacher stuff. Sweatshirts, mugs, magnets with apples and sayings like, "2 teach is 2 touch a life 4ever." I was going into the inner city in an eighth grade classroom and somehow that style didn't seem to fit the environment I was entering. I thought I needed to be tough and an apple sweatshirt was not going to cut it.

I taught in Columbus, Ohio for two years. I worked with amazing people and had a wonderful experience. A job opportunity became available in the area where I grew up and being the girl that I am, I had to move back to family. I have been working in Canfield, Ohio for ten years.

My experience ranges from the inner city to an affluent community, from a first grade classroom to an auditorium at the university level. I've had the eager and the at-risk all in the same class. I've faced budget cuts, shared a classroom due to overcrowding, and taught my first year from an overhead cart in any space that was free for a class period.

Throughout all of these experiences I am thrilled to say that I finally have my mission statement; To touch a life forever. I know what you're thinking, "You got that off a sweatshirt!" Well, there is a reason those things sell like hotcakes! I have decided to make a difference on purpose, not by accident. Each day I walk into my classroom, and I see hundreds of people, students, staff and parents. All of them, like me, can be changed or touched with one life-producing exchange, a smile, a compliment, a positive note sent home. The list is endless.

I look for ways to bring out the gold in everyone I encounter. I have to say, I didn't learn that in a college class. I learned that from my parents who were both teachers. The memories they share about the classroom have never been about dynamic lessons. No. They are about the kids. They loved what they did because they loved who they taught. I am so grateful to both of them for showing me that it's not all about test scores, it's

Out of relationship, everything else will prosper.

all about relationship. Out of relationship, everything else will prosper.

I have been honored to join Pastor Thomas as he compiled stories from his life about how teachers have impacted who he is today. He represents the voice that I choose to hear every day as I walk into my school. The voice that I choose to listen to throughout the year when test scores are breathing down my neck or during third period when the student I've been helping decides to blow off the assignment.

I am making a difference. How do I know? It's in the little things. It's in the way Ryan says he's never had a teacher believe in him. It's in the way that Sami, who was labeled as a difficult girl, screams my name in the mall to say hi. It's in the way I get a thank you note from Alex who says she never heard a teacher say she loved her before. I don't own one of those sweatshirts, but it coins a phrase that has inspired me throughout the years. To teach is to touch a life forever.

The other day I was in the media center and our librarian had this statement posted on her computer. She wasn't sure where it came from, but I believe this statement is somewhat the moral of the story. I leave it with you and encourage you to let this resonate within.

They will not always remember what you taught them, but they will remember how you treated them.

Keep making a difference,

Michelle DeFabio

About the Author

David L. Thomas sees his family as his greatest joy. He has had the privilege of being married to his childhood sweetheart Kathie since 1972.

Their two grown children, Heather (Varnell) and David Jonathan, as well as their three grandchildren Ethan, Alaina, and Anna are their special delight and legacy.

Over his career, David has developed into a leader of leaders and his influence reaches people from all walks of life. He serves on the board of several international ministries as he influences others to go further, fly higher, and enjoy the journey!

As a minister, life coach, conference speaker, network leader and author, his goal is to inspire others through passion and humor, to love God completely, love others unconditionally, and love life enthusiastically!

Get More Inspiration

A TEACHER'S GIFT is an excellent gift choice for a teacher, friend or anyone who influences others.

Visit **www.aTeachersGift.com** now to order additional hard copies. The web site offers even more sources of inspiration.

It's the author's pleasure to offer quantity discounts to schools, school districts, PTA and PTO, and other non-profit organizations.